James Curtis Wedlake.

Little Church,
June 8th, 1919.

DAVID AS A GOOD SHEPHERD

Little Folks Series

Little Folks of The Bible

BY

DOROTHY DONNELL CALHOUN

Book II

BOYS IN THE DAYS OF THE PROPHETS

DAVID	DANIEL
SAMUEL	THE SHUNAMMITE'S SON

THE ABINGDON PRESS
NEW YORK   CINCINNATI

CONTENTS

ILLUSTRATIONS

INTRODUCTION

"THE proper study of mankind," said Pope, tersely and wisely, "is man." To twist his phrase a bit, may we not say that the proper study of childkind is children? It is with this idea that I have attempted in these little stories to picture the childhood of some of the heroes and heroines of the Bible for the children of to-day.

It has been my aim to make these little folks of the long ago *real* little folks, studying, laughing, playing, grieving as boys and girls do now. The Bible itself, of course, has furnished most of the facts for the stories, although ancient Jewish histories and commentaries have supplemented the Bible source. A few of the selections, "Paul's Nephew," for example, and "The Boy of the Loaves and Fishes," are fanciful tales woven about incidents in the New Testament. In none of them,

INTRODUCTION

I trust, have the spirit and teachings of the Book of books been violated.

To most children's minds the Bible seems a record of events that happened very long ago. It is possible that in many cases the strange old customs and the characteristic Bible phraseology may divert the child's mind from the truths of the Bible, which are as vital and pertinent to-day as in the long ago. Possibly—I do not say in all cases—Samson and his jawbone, David and his sling, and Daniel among the lions may appear to young students as storybook people who never really lived at all.

But children believe in the experiences of other children. Young David watching his father's sheep, the little daughter of Jephtha with her songs and household tasks, the pure-eyed Child-Jesus toiling in the humble carpenter's shop in Nazareth —these are comprehensible to children. Introduced to these characters as children, their later lives become vivid and full of interest. They are friends, *real* people.

8

INTRODUCTION

While Bible stories for children are not a new thing, very few, if any, of these stories have attempted precisely the thing that has been attempted in these little books. They are not the tales of the great deeds or the great heroes of the Old and New Testament, but the stories of real children for real children to read.

DOROTHY DONNELL CALHOUN.

9

BOYS IN THE DAYS OF THE PROPHETS

DAVID
SAMUEL
THE SHUNAMMITE'S SON
DANIEL

DAVID

NEAR the little village of Bethlehem, more than a thousand years before Christ was born, there lived an old man named Jesse and his eight tall, handsome sons. Seven of the sons were grown men and knew how to draw a bow and throw a spear like trained soldiers; but the youngest, David, was still a child, though strong and large for his age. And because he was too young to learn to hunt and fight, like his brothers, he was given the care of his father's flocks of sheep and goats on the hillsides above the sleepy little town.

From near and far about Bethlehem came the news of war. The Philistines, a race of fierce and terrible warriors, were marching across the borders of their land to attack the Hebrews. The Hebrew king, Saul, men said, had disobeyed the will of God and was no longer to be trusted to lead his people on to victory. In his palace, with his wives about him, he sulked his time away, while everywhere, in town and countryside, his people trembled with terror and dread. But David, watching his woolly flocks on the steep, lonely hillsides, did not hear the echo of far-away battles. Instead, the wild mountains and rocky valleys rang to the sound of his fresh young voice, or the throb of his harp strings under his skillful finger-tips. The beautiful green pasture land about Bethlehem, dotted here and there with white sheep, was the boy's world. He knew nothing of the life of the court, the cities, the battlefield, and had no wish to know of them.

Sometimes great mountains or views of the sea, stretching away to meet the sky, bring great thoughts to men. Perhaps it was like this with David, the shepherd boy. Later, when he grew to be a man, he wrote some of the most wonderful psalms that have ever been read or sung, and even here in his lonely childhood on the bare mountainsides his fingers would often wan-der across the strings of his little harp and he would sing the thoughts that filled his soul. The outdoor life made him strong and vigorous, with the muscles and the hardiness of a grown man.

Although Jesse, the father, was a humble peasant and poor, he was a man of good character, who brought up his family to serve and worship God. So most of the simple little songs the boy David made up and sang while tending his sheep and goats were in praise of God's goodness and mercy toward men.

Yet, although the life on the hills was quiet and peaceful, there was sometimes danger even here—danger, not from armed men, but from wild beasts that crept down among the rocks to steal the lambs. David had no sword to help him drive such enemies away, but he had a quick mind, a love of adventure, and a sturdy courage, which, after all, are as good as weapons oftentimes. In a shepherd's bag he always carried a number of smooth, round stones from the bed of the brook, and at his belt hung a sling.

Once a lion attacked his flock and started to carry away a tiny newborn lamb. The boy placed a stone in his sling, drew it back, and struck the great, tawny beast on the head, so that he fell down to the ground. Then David ran up fearlessly, drew the lamb unhurt from the cruel jaws, and when the beast would have seized him he held him by the mane and killed him. At another time a hungry bear, pouncing upon the flock, met the same fate. And so, guarding the sheep, singing and playing on his harp, David passed his days in the pastures of Bethlehem, while beyond the hills his countrymen fell beneath the blows of the terrible Philistines.

At last something happened to break the quiet of his life. The prophet Samuel, an old, bent man, white-haired and very wise, came one day to the village, bringing with him a white heifer. When the towns-people questioned him the prophet said that he had come to sacrifice the heifer in the town. But really his errand was much greater, for he had come there under the direction of the Lord to seek a king for Israel. Saul, the present king, had disobeyed the will of God and was no longer worthy to rule; the enemy was camped on the very borders of the land; and the poor people had no leader and were helpless and afraid.

"God will give the kingdom to a better man than you," Samuel had told King Saul, sadly, and now he had come down to Bethlehem seeking a man of the family of the peasant Jesse to be the next king. So he invited Jesse and his sons to the sacrifice and to the feast afterward. About the board, heaped with raisin cakes, figs, bread, and jugs of wine, sat the old, white-bearded father and his seven grown sons, each one tall, handsome, and kingly-looking; yet, as he gazed from one to the other, Samuel shook his head. The man that he sought for the future king of Israel was not there.

"Are all your children here?" he asked Jesse at last.

"The youngest, David, keeps the sheep," answered the father.

"Send for him," said Samuel.

Soon the boy stood before him, ruddy, fair-haired, sturdy of limb, holding his harp beneath his arm and his sling in one hand.

The prophet looked at him a long time in solemn joy, and, lifting his horn of sacred oil, he poured it upon the boy's curls, saying, "This is he, the future king."

The father and brothers watched in amazement. They could hardly believe that they had heard right. What! Their little David, tender of goats, unbearded, and a child, *he* a king? No! Impossible! Yet so the holy man had said. He was promising him a long, useful life, fame, wealth, a great name. They did not understand.

"Say nothing of what has happened," Samuel told them. "It will be many years before it comes to pass."

And, so speaking, he went away. But the world had changed for David, and life could never be quite the same hereafter. Often now he left his flocks in the care of a keeper and went to Ramah, the home town of Samuel, to visit the old man. There he learned how to play other instruments besides the harp, and how to read and sing. And, better than these things, the old man would often speak to him of God and his purposes, so that David's faith grew stronger every day.

Now, while all these strange, new things had been happening to young David at Gibeah, the court of King Saul, there was grief and anxiety, for the king was very ill with an unknown sickness that made him brood for hours without speaking, then suddenly rage and curse, until his servants whispered that a demon must be torturing him.

The doctors could do nothing to cure him; even the news of the enemy's nearness did not arouse him. At last one doctor told the king that if he could find some one to play on the harp and sing to him the music might soothe him, and perhaps he would get well.

"Find me a harp-player," Saul commanded his attendants.

"I have seen such a one in Bethlehem, O king," said one. "He is David, the son of Jesse, a child in years, but comely, good, and well-skilled in harp-playing and hymn-singing."

And so it happened that soon after a messenger arrived in Bethlehem with an order to Jesse from King Saul, "Send me your son David, who is with the sheep."

Jesse loaded an ass with bread, a bottle of wine, and a kid, and sent his youngest boy with these gifts to the king. And for the first time in his life David saw the splendor of the court and the glitter of breastplates and swords in the sun. The winning ways of the peasant lad soon won the hearts of all the court, from gloomy King Saul down to the poorest of the servants. Every day he went to the tent where the king lay ill and played and sang so sweetly to him that he calmed his fits of gloom and made him well. Saul grew so fond of the boy that he was unwilling to have him out of his sight for long and made him his armor-bearer. Indeed, he loved him almost as well as he did his own son, Jonathan. As for Jonathan—a gentle, frank boy of about David's own age—the youth, beauty, and power of the shepherd boy won his heart at once, and between the two children there grew up a warm, generous friendship that was to last all their lives. Jonathan shared all his belongings with David, even his own robe, girdle, bow and shield, and loved him "as his own soul."

But now the great army of the Philistines had come very near to the capital indeed, and harp-playing was drowned in the rattle of armor and the din of war. So Saul sent young David back to the safety of his father's roof, and led his army out to meet the enemy. The Philistines encamped on one high hill, the Hebrews on another. Opposite and between the two armies stretched a valley, green, peaceful, still. Down into this valley every morning marched a gigantic figure, a Philistine soldier named Goliath, ten feet tall and broad and sturdy as an oak tree. A brass helmet and coat of mail weighing hundreds of pounds covered his head and body and clanked loudly as he walked. Before him and behind went armor-bearers staggering under the weight of his great spear and shield as large as a roof. He was one of four giant brothers from the city of Gath, and the very sight of him was enough to fill the hearts of smaller men with dread.

When he reached the center of the valley facing the Hebrew camp Goliath stood still, the sun striking sparks of light from his shining armor, and shouted these words: "Choose a man from among you and let him come down to me. If he be able to fight with me and to kill me, then will we be your servants; but if I kill him, then you shall be our servants. Give me a man, that we may fight together."

The great voice of the giant boomed like thunder among the hills, but when the echoes had died away there was no answer from the Hebrew camp, for no one dared to go down to meet the terrible Philistine, armed as he was from head to foot and tall as two men.

DAVID

And so Goliath marched back again to his own camp. But every day he returned to shout his challenge, and every day the Hebrews trembled and were afraid to answer him. In vain Saul begged and commanded his men, and promised rich rewards and the hand of one of his daughters to the man who would fight Goliath and win. Life was too dear to each soldier for him to fling it carelessly away. And in all the Hebrew camp there was no one equal in size to the giant Philistine.

Meanwhile in Bethlehem a shadow of anxiety lay over the home of Jesse, for three of the grown sons had gone away to fight with the Hebrew army and the people at home had not heard a word from them since they had left. On the hillsides David watched the sheep as before, but this time a war-note crept into the songs he sang and his eyes were often turned in the direction of Elah, where he knew the two armies were gathered. It seemed a little hard to him to have to stay tamely in a pasture with only goats and sheep about him while over the hills his brothers were fighting to defend their country. Yet he did his work faithfully without complaining, and soon his chance came.

His father called the lad to him and showed him an ass loaded with food. "To-morrow you shall carry this parched corn and these ten loaves of bread to your brothers in the camp of Saul," he said. "And these ten cheeses to their captain, and inquire how they all are and how the battle is going."

As soon as the first faint light came through David's window the next morning he was awake and dressed ready for his journey. He left the sheep in the care of another keeper and set out joyfully to Elah, leading the loaded ass. At last he came to the camp and found his brothers. As he distributed the gifts he had brought with him, and stood talking to the three, Goliath marched down from the camp of the Philistines with a great clatter of armor and stood below in the valley, jeering at the Hebrews as cowards because none dared come down and fight.

David listened, his cheeks growing red with anger at the scornful words, then turned to his brothers, clenching his hands.

"I am ready to fight alone with this man!" he cried.

The soldiers standing near looked first at the slender, unarmed boy, and then down at the giant, and laughed. But his brothers were very angry, and reproved him for boasting.

"Why did you come here?" cried Eliab, the oldest. "I know the naughtiness of your heart. You came to see the battle. Go home at once to your sheep."

David turned sadly away, but one of the soldiers who had heard his brave words and believed them went to King Saul and told him of the slender lad who wished to fight the giant of the Philistines. Surprised and amused, Saul sent for him, and lo! there was his own little harpist and armor-bearer bowing before the throne!

"You are only a youth," said the king,

gently. "You are not able to fight this man of war."

David's eyes flashed. "O king," he cried, "I will fight with him, tall as he is and great as he is, and your army shall get great glory when he shall be slain by a child."

"No, no," sighed the king. "You are too weak and young."

"God will be with me," said David, firmly. "He has helped me already to kill a savage lion that was carrying away one of my lambs, and a fierce bear."

The king was amazed at the boy's boldness and courage, and suddenly decided to let him try his skill, although his heart was troubled, for he loved the boy, and it seemed almost certain that he would be killed.

"Go to the fight," he commanded, solemnly. Then he took off his own royal breastplate, sword, and helmet and fastened them on the boy. The steel armor was so heavy that David could hardly move in it. His hand fell at his side seeking his shepherd sling.

"I do not know how to use these heavy things, O king," cried he, laying aside the mail. "But do not fear for me. I have my weapon here." And he took five smooth, round stones and his sling and went out to meet the giant foe, leaving the king praying for his success.

For forty days Goliath had come down into the valley to hurl his challenge, and gone back again to his own camp without fighting. So it is no wonder when he first saw young David coming down the hill to meet him that he laughed aloud until the hills echoed his mirth—a child, golden-haired as a girl, unarmed except for the rude shepherd sling in one hand! So this was the champion of the Hebrews! Such a one surely would not be hard to slay.

"Do you take me not for a man, but for a dog, boy?" he jeered, pointing to the sling.

"No!" cried David, fiercely, fitting one of the stones into his weapon. "Not for a dog, but for a creature worse than a dog!"

The words angered the giant, who lifted his spear, tall as a fir tree, and came toward the boy, slowly because of the great weight of his armor, but shouting threats and curses as he came.

"You have a sword and spear and shield," cried David, fearlessly raising his sling, "but God is with me and he will defeat you!"

The stone flew from the sling, straight and true as an arrow, striking Goliath in the center of the forehead, so that he fell crashing to the ground. Lifting the giant's own sword, David cut off the mighty head and held it up for the watching armies to see. When the Philistines knew that their greatest soldier had been killed by a boy with a pebble from a brook they lost their courage and fled back to their own country in terror of their lives. Saul's army followed them, tearing down their tents and forts and killing many before they could escape. But David went back alone to the king. He laid the fierce head at the foot of the throne and went quietly away without waiting for Saul to praise him or reward him, as though he had done nothing at all strange or brave. But the king, looking down at the head of his mighty foe, and hearing the shouts of his army cheering the boy-hero, and the songs of the women praising the shepherd lad, suddenly felt troubled and afraid, for he remembered how, long ago, the prophet Samuel had told him that a better man than he should rule over Israel, and he wondered whether David could be that better man.

But David went back to his father's flocks and his wild mountain pastures, forgetting for a while the rattle of armor or the din of the camp. He could not look ahead far down his manhood years and see the crown that awaited him or the glory that was to be added to his name. And so he sang his psalms as in the old days and watched the white sheep, the stern mountains, and the calm blue sky. But wherever he went he felt God with him, and so succeeded in all he had to do.

LITTLE FOLKS OF THE BIBLE

Now It's Your Turn

1. What was David's family like? How many brothers had he? How old were they?

2. What was David's work? What did he like to do as he watched the sheep? On what instruments did he play? What did he sing about?

3. Tell the story of David and the lion and the bear.

4. Who was Samuel? What did he do? Tell the story of the feast and what happened there.

5. How did the doctor say Saul could be cured? Who did they get to cure him? How did the court like David? How did Saul like him? What lifelong friend did he make there?

6. Tell about the war. Who were the Philistines? Who was their champion? Describe him.

7. How did David happen to go to camp? What did he hear there? What did he wish to do? How did the brothers like his words?

DAVID

8. What did Saul say? What did David reply? Why did David not wear the king's armor? What weapons did he use?

9. Tell about the fight between David and Goliath and the result. Why was the king afraid? What did David do after his victory?

10. What did David become in after years? What sort of a boy was David? What sort of a man did he grow to be? What were some of the things he did and wrote in after life?

SAMUEL

AFTER the Hebrew people had lived many, many years in Egypt, and had been ill treated and abused by the cruel kings, or Pharaohs that ruled the land, they left the country in a great body and journeyed up through the wilderness to Canaan. Here their ancestors, Abraham, Isaac, and Jacob, had lived, and here they hoped to find a peaceful home once more. Moses was the leader of the company, and they started out joyfully with songs and praises. The journey lasted forty years. At last, discouraged and weary, they came to the promised land. Here they separated into twelve divisions, or tribes, each one the descendants of one of Jacob's twelve sons. And here too they set up their tabernacle and placed in it the most valuable thing they had brought with them from Egypt. This was the ark of God.

The ark was a box, or chest, made of a

wood called "shittim," five feet long, three feet broad and high. It was covered with gold outside and inside, and had four golden rings at the corners to carry it by. Inside this box were kept the stone tablets on which Moses had written the laws of God. The tabernacle in which the ark was kept was a movable tent covered with ram's skin dyed red and hung with many blue and scarlet curtains. They had built this tent and ark in the wilderness at God's command and had carried it wherever they went.

Now that they had at last reached the end of their wanderings, they chose a place called Shiloh, in the green valleys of Canaan, and set up their tabernacle there, this time to stay. Here they came to pray and to offer up sacrifices to God.

But the new country was a large place, with mountains and stretches of desert. Some of the tribes of Israelites lived a long way from Shiloh, among strange people who did not worship the one true God. Instead they set up ugly images of brass

and bronze, some with the face of a man
and the body of a fish, whom they called
Dagon, and some with rams' horns or bulls'
heads, whom they called Baal. These
images were worshiped with terrible ceremonies, in which human beings were killed
and injured, while dancing and drinking
much wine were a part. At first the Israelites would have nothing to do with
these heathen images, but remembered
God's laws and were true to his worship
alone. But the tribes were so scattered
that they seldom met together, and the
rulers, who were called judges, could not
reach or unite them. And little by little
some of the furthest tribes began to do as
their heathen neighbors did, forgetting the
ark and the tabernacle that were so far
away. Then wars and troubles began to
come. The stranger nations who lived in
Canaan were not always friendly, and some
of the tribes had to fight for their very
lives.

Years passed by; the sanctuary still stood
at Shiloh, and a body of holy men called

Levites guarded the ark, as their fathers had done. Still sacrifices smoked on the altar in the temple and worshipers came daily to bring offerings and to pray. For, though some of the Israelites had begun to worship heathen images, there were very many others who remained true to the religion their forefathers had brought up out of Egypt, and who left their farms and vineyards every year to travel to Shiloh and worship there. Some of them brought rich offerings, some poor ones, but all brought something to lay before God's altars as a sacrifice—oil, spices, gold, rams, bulls, lambs, even bread and flour and wine.

Among the faithful was a man named Elkanah, who lived at Ramah, near Mount Ephraim, with his two wives, Peninnah and Hannah. Peninnah had many sons and daughters, but Hannah had none, and sometimes Peninnah would boast to the other wife about her own children and would sneer at her unkindly because she did not have any herself. Poor Hannah was very unhappy, for she loved children and wanted a son more than anything else in the world. She often prayed for one, but years went by and still her prayers were unanswered. Her husband tried to comfort her, telling her that she had him to love, but still she mourned for a son.

Now Elkanah was a good man. Every year with his wives and children he traveled up to Shiloh and offered up one of his lambs or goats as a sacrifice. One year, at the feast after the sacrifice, Elkanah, when he came to divide the meat and wine, gave Peninnah and her sons and daughters an equal share of the food, but to Hannah he gave more than to any of the rest, for he loved Hannah very dearly. Peninnah saw this and was angry, so she began to taunt Hannah again because she had no children. The unkind words and her own grief made Hannah weep so that she could not eat any of the bread or meat before her or drink the wine. After the feast was over she left the others and went to the temple, where she began to pray silently. She

promised God that if he would send her a
son she would bring the boy up in God's
service, not in the evil ways of other men.

As Hannah prayed a priest of the temple
named Eli, a Levite, watched her. When she
was going away he told her that her prayer
would be answered very soon. And, sure
enough, the next year a boy baby was
born to Hannah, and she named him Samuel, which means in the Hebrew language
"Asked of God."

Of course, the first year the baby was too
young to go to Shiloh when his father went
to offer his yearly sacrifice, but Hannah
promised that as soon as Samuel was old
enough she would take him to the tabernacle herself and leave him there, as she
had vowed to God. So during his baby-
hood Samuel lived at Ramah and learned
to talk and to repeat the prayers his mother
said to him. As soon as he could walk
about and take care of himself his mother
took three bullocks, a sack of flour, and a
bottle of wine, set her son on the back of
an ass, and went to Shiloh with her hus-

band. Although she felt sad at having to give up her boy, she was proud and happy to think she had such a son, and that he would grow up to be a priest and a prophet.

At Shiloh the parents killed a bullock as a sacrifice and took Samuel to the tabernacle. There sat old Eli, the priest, as Hannah had seen him sitting when she went to pray for her child several years before.

"My lord," said Hannah, bowing very low before the old, white-haired man, "I am the woman that once stood here by you praying for this child to be given me. God heard me, and so I have brought him here to lend him to the Lord as long as he lives."

Then she bade the boy good-by and went home to Ramah with her husband. And the little boy stayed with Eli, who taught him many new things—to help with the sacrifices and to take care of all the dishes and furnishings of the tabernacle. At first his new home seemed very strange to Samuel after his father's house at Ramah, with its courtyard garden and playground on the roof, fenced in with battlements. The tabernacle where he now lived was a big tent, oblong in shape, with a wooden framework covered over with gaily-colored cloth and skins of the camel and the ram. Inside the tent were two rooms, divided from each other by a curtain, or veil, made of blue, purple, and scarlet linen. On the curtain were pictures of angels and cherubim woven into the cloth. Samuel used to look often at the strange pictures and admire the bright colors of the veil.

The inner room was a small one called the Holy of holies, because the sacred ark was kept there. Little Samuel was never allowed even to peep into this room, for it was never opened except on the day of atonement, and then only Eli himself could go in. But the old priest told the boy about the tablets of stone that were kept in the ark, and what laws and commandments were written on them, until the child knew almost as much as the old man about the teachings of God.

The outer room was much larger. It was called the Holy Place, or Sanctuary, where people came to worship and pray every day. Here little Samuel spent much of his time opening and closing the doors of the temple every morning and evening, caring for the altar, and helping the priests with the rites of worship. In this room was a table inlaid with gold and covered with bowls and spoons of gold, and with a great golden candlestick in the center. On this table the people placed the twelve loaves of bread that they brought every week for the priests to eat, and cakes made of wheat flour and oil. Here in this room was also the altar where sweet incense was always kept burning. Sometimes Samuel was allowed to fill the lamps on the altar in the morning and to light them in the evening.

Beside the tabernacle were the tents where the priests lived and where Samuel ate and slept and grew from childhood into boyhood peacefully and happily. Once every year his father and mother came to Shiloh. Then Hannah brought with her a

little coat that she had woven for her son.
Sometimes his father came alone, and told
the boy that he had a new baby sister or
brother at home, for Hannah had many
other sons and daughters after Samuel
came to Shiloh. But Samuel never left the
temple to visit his people, and did not see
Ramah again until he was a grown man.

Almost the only people whom he did see
were those who came to worship, and the
priests themselves, dressed in their strange
coats, or ephods, as they were called, made
of gold, blue and red linen, with chains and
rings of gold and jewels, and tall golden
caps called miters on their heads. He himself was too young to wear all this splendor.
His own dress was a short linen robe reach-
ing to his knees and belted in at the waist.
He wore his hair long, as the priests did,
and lived very simply, eating no sweet-
meats, drinking water instead of wine, and
sleeping on a thin mattress spread on the
ground.

Since he was the only child in the temple
among so many wise, white-haired old men,

Samuel must have been rather a grave, silent boy, who thought more than he laughed, and worked rather than played. He spent much time in study and in prayer and did his tasks faithfully and well. Sometimes he spent whole nights in the Holy Place watching the altar fires, which were never allowed to go out, filling the lamps with olive oil, and burning the incense on the altar. Here he thought many solemn thoughts and dreamed many strange dreams. He thought of the teachings in the tablets of the law, the sacrifices that men offered, and wondered whether God really wished rams and sheep as offerings, or human hearts and lives devoted to doing good. The thought that some of the Israelites were worshiping strange heathen images and becoming wicked was a dreadful one to the boy, and there was another thing that troubled him.

Eli, his best friend, had two sons, grown men, whose lives were so wicked that they made their old father very sad. Samuel had often heard Eli begging them to be

SAMUEL

better men and warning them that God would punish them for their sins. But they did not listen and went on doing wrong as before. Samuel pitied his old friend for his wicked sons, and wondered whether God would indeed punish them.

One night, when he was twelve years old, a strange thing happened. Just as he was ready to go to sleep Samuel thought he heard a voice calling out to him. He jumped up and ran to where Eli was lying, crying: "You called me. Here I am."

"No, no," said the old priest, "I did not speak. Go back and lie down."

The boy went back to his mattress and tried to sleep, but again he seemed to hear a voice crying, "Samuel! Samuel!"

Once more he sprang out of bed and went to Eli, and once more the old man sent him away. The third time the voice came Samuel was almost frightened when Eli shook his head.

"Indeed, my child, I was silent now as before," he said, slowly. "Perhaps God was speaking to you. The next time you hear the call answer, "I am here."

"Samuel! Samuel! Samuel!" the boy seemed to hear again.

"Speak," he cried. "I am listening."

And then, although the words were not said aloud, Samuel thought he heard a far-away voice say sternly: "Misery is coming upon the Israelites. Eli's sons must die because they have sinned and he has not stopped them."

The words died away. The poor little boy lay wide awake until morning, thinking sadly about what he had heard and feeling very sorrowful because he had to tell his good old friend Eli such terrible news. When morning came he got up, dressed, and opened the doors of the temple without speaking to the priests about what he had heard in the night. Then Eli called him, and he went with a sinking heart.

"Here I am," he answered with a sad face.

"Tell me what God said to you in the

night," said the old man. "Do not keep anything from me."

So Samuel told Eli what he had heard. The old priest said only, "Let the Lord do as He wills."

But the boy could see that his heart was breaking.

Time went on. Samuel had other visions and heard other words. He told them to the priests and the people who came to worship, and they all were surprised to hear a boy saying such things. They remembered what he told them, and saw that it all came true. So they knew then that Samuel was going to be a great prophet some day and listened eagerly to everything he said.

And before many years both of Eli's sons were killed in a battle with the Philistines. Worse than that, the ark of God, which the army had carried with it to bring them victory, was stolen by the enemy. When Eli heard these dreadful tidings he fell over, striking his neck, and died. So Samuel was left alone in the temple to tell the people of the will of God, for none of the other priests knew as much as he.

He served God faithfully all his life, and when he was a grown man he united all the scattered tribes of Israel under one king, Saul, and, better still, under the worship of the one true God. He lived to be an old, old man, and to anoint David as king also, before he died, loved and honored by all his people, at Ramah, his birthplace among the hills.

I Know—See Whether You Do

1. Why did the Israelites leave Egypt? Who was their leader? Where did they go? How long were they on the way?

2. What did they bring with them? What was the ark of God? What was the tabernacle? Where did they put these?

3. How did the Israelites divide up the new country? What sort of people were their neighbors? What gods did they worship? Did the Israelites forget their own religion?

4. What were the names of the priests of

the tabernacle? What did many of the Israelites do every year? What sort of offerings did they bring?

5. What were the names of Samuel's parents? What was the name of the other wife? Why was Hannah unhappy? What did she wish? Where did she pray for her wish? Who was there when she prayed?

6. What did Hannah do with Samuel when he was a little boy? What sort of a place was his new home? What was the Holy of holies? Who entered?

7. Describe the rest of the tabernacle. What were the furnishings? What were some of Samuel's duties? What did he learn? How often did he see his parents?

8. What did the priests wear? Eat? Where did they live? What sort of a boy was Samuel?

9. What did he hear when he was twelve years old? What had the sons of Eli done? What did Eli say when Samuel told his vision? Was it true?

10. What did Samuel become? What did he do in life? Where did he die?

DANIEL

IT was more than one thousand years after the Hebrews had come up into Canaan from Egypt that this story happened. A great many things can happen in a thousand years. The twelve tribes that had at first settled in Canaan had divided into two larger groups called Judah and Israel, and one of these groups, Israel, which contained ten of the original twelve tribes, had been taken captive by its enemies and carried away. From that day no one ever heard of the Ten Lost Tribes again. So there remained of the Hebrew race in Canaan only the tribe of Judah, which occupied the land where, in the far-away times, Abraham and Isaac and Jacob had lived and died. Jerusalem was the capital city of Judah, and here most of the Hebrews lived.

But even this last tribe was not safe. Far to the east, across the great Syrian desert, lay the powerful and greedy country of Assyria. The king of one part of Assyria—Babylon—was Nebuchadnezzar, a great soldier and ruler who desired to leave his country rich and famous when he died. After he had conquered many of the lands and cities in his own part of the world he sent his armies far and wide across the desert to conquer the Jews also. At first he attacked only the country places and the smaller towns, but the Jews, watching the terrible strength of the Assyrian forces from behind the walls of the capital, trembled for fear that Jerusalem would be the next place to be taken. They tried to make the walls of the city safer and to lay up plenty of food in the storehouses; then they called as many of the Jewish people as possible into the city and waited. And, sure enough, presently the great army of Babylonians appeared before the walls and began to attack Jerusalem. Nebuchadnezzar built great towers of stone beside the walls, and from the tops of these the enemy threw spears and shot arrows into the city.

He raised outer walls around the capital walls and fought from these.

Inside Jerusalem the men and women did not lose their courage at the danger. They went about their work, took care of the soldiers who were hurt by the darts and arrows of the Assyrians, and prayed for victory. But some of them prayed to idols and some to God, for many of the Jews had almost forgotten the religion of their fathers and were beginning to worship the strange, hideous images and figures that their neighbors, the heathen nations, bowed down to. Those who remained true to the teachings of their race looked at the idol-worship of their brothers in horror and cried aloud that God would surely punish such wickedness.

A group of men called prophets sprang up. These were preachers and teachers, who went about trying to get men to return to the worship of the one true God and to leave incense and ugly wood and stone images alone. The prophets saw Jerusalem surrounded on all sides by fierce soldiers from a foreign land, and they believed that here was the punishment God was sending on the race for their disloyalty and sin.

But still the siege went on, and still Jerusalem was not taken. The people in the city fought bravely, but their food was almost gone, and a grave sickness had come upon the city, killing many of the weaker ones. At last, after eighteen months of defense, the poor Jews opened their gates and the Babylonians marched in. Nebuchadnezzar ordered the temple which had been built by King Solomon four hundred years before to be torn down, after the soldiers had taken everything of worth from it. Gold and silver dishes, gold tables and candlesticks and brass pillars were taken out and carried away to Babylon, where they were put into the temples of the heathen gods there. The palace and houses of the cities were destroyed and the walls torn down. Then, taking about seven hundred of the noble Jews as prisoners, the Babylonian army marched home.

LITTLE FOLKS OF THE BIBLE

Among the Jewish prisoners were a number of children belonging to the families of the princes and royalty. These children were chosen for their beauty of face and figure, their quickness of mind and their pleasant dispositions. They were all boys, and all of them fine, tall, brave lads, such as any nation might be proud to own. Over the desert and mountains went the army and the prisoners, coming at last to the green, fertile land of Babylon in the valley of the Euphrates River. The great river rushed along between low and level banks, wild with the melting snows that it brought down from the mountains far away in Asia, dark and very wide. The Jews looked about them with wonder when they saw the city of Babylon, for two kings had spent their lives in making it strong and beautiful, until now it was a very marvel city which could surely never be captured by any army in the world.

Nebuchadnezzar had built three walls of brick, with beautiful cedar wood gates, decorated with bronze, and statues of gods and men. He had built another palace for himself, higher and larger than any building in the city, and filled it with silver, gold, and statues. Around the building he had erected high stone walls so wide that many men could walk on them. Here he planted trees and flowers like a hanging park. The streets of the city were broad and well paved and there were bridges, canals, and temples everywhere. Babylon was one of the most beautiful cities in the world, and even the Jews had to admire it. Most of the prisoners, the men and women, were given homes of their own in the new city, with lands, camels, horses, mules, and asses, and here they settled down to live as though they had never left their home country. But Nebuchadnezzar kept the children with him in the palace.

Among the Jewish boys were four who were great friends. They belonged to the Jews who had remained faithful to the true God of their fathers and looked with horror at the bronze and stone images that the king and the other Babylonians prayed to. One of these boys was named Daniel, the others were Hananiah, Mishael, and Azariah. The king was very much pleased with the beauty, good tempers, and quick wits of the four, but he treated them no better than he did the rest, who were all good and clever children. He gave them teachers, and commanded that they should be taught to write in the characters of the Assyrians, to read and to speak the language of the new country.

Daniel and his three friends were very glad to learn all they could, and studied so hard and so well that they were soon ahead of the other children. They learned the new science of mathematics and figures, how to tell the names and places of the stars, the sciences, the history of Assyria, and many other things that they never could have known if they had stayed in Jerusalem, for numbers and real writing and the sciences were not taught there. Now and then the king would ask the teachers how the Jewish children were getting along in their studies, and he was delighted to hear of

their progress. But there was one thing
that troubled Daniel.

Nebuchadnezzar was so fond of the
stranger children that he sent them food
from his own table. It was rich, heavy
food—meats, spiced pastry, wine, and cakes;
and Daniel had been taught not to eat
these things. Some of them were forbidden
by the Jewish laws, and some were so rich
that they made him feel very dull and
unable to think quickly. He and his
friends had been brought up simply on
fruit, grain, and milk and cheese. Instead
of liking the new, strange things they were
given to eat, they hated them. So Daniel
resolved not to eat the king's food any
longer.

He went to the head of the servants
whom the king had told to take care of
the children. This man's name was Melzar,
and he was very fond of Daniel because of
his pleasant ways and kindness even to
servants.

"Melzar," said Daniel, coaxingly, "I and
my three friends do not like the food that

the king sends us to eat. It is too rich, and, besides, we have been taught at home not to eat meat or to drink wine. Will you please get us something else?"

Melzar looked doubtful and shook his head. "I am afraid the king will be angry if I do," he said. "When he sees that you are thinner and paler than the rest of the children he will punish me for not taking better care of you."

"No, no," cried Daniel. "The king will never know. Try giving us four what we wish for ten days, and at the end of that time see whether we do not look as well as the rest."

"But what will I do with the food that the king sends you?" asked Melzar. "And what do you wish to eat?"

"You shall have the food yourself," said Daniel. "And as for us, we want only pulse and water, or any other grain and fruit you wish, but no meat or wine."

So Melzar agreed to try for ten days what the boy suggested. He took the dishes of rich food that were brought from the king's banquet table and gave them to the other servants and to the rest of the Jewish children; but to Daniel and his friends he gave dates, vegetables, and water, as they had asked. At the end of ten days he called all of the children together, looked at them, and, sure enough, Daniel, Hananiah, Mishael, and Azariah were fat and rosy, indeed much fatter and rosier than the other children who had been eating the king's food. They were brighter in their minds too, and had been able to study far more than the rest. So the servant took away the meat and wine from all of the children and gave them the pulse and fruit instead.

At the end of three years the king sent for the children to be brought before him. The servants who had the care of them led them into the throne room, and Nebuchadnezzar looked at them and talked to them. He asked questions about history, mathematics, and science, and of all of the boys Daniel and his friends answered the best. The king called the four to him and asked their names. When they had told them, Nebuchadnezzar shook his head. He could not say the strange Jewish words.

"I shall give you Assyrian names," he told them. So he called Mishael Meshach; Azariah, Abed-nego; Hananiah, Shadrach. But to Daniel, whom he liked above all the others, the king gave the name Belteshazzar, which was a great honor in his mind, for Belteshazzar was the name of the favorite god whom Nebuchadnezzar worshiped.

Already Daniel knew about the strange gods of the Babylonians. He had been to the temples, which were great brick buildings decorated with the beautiful things that the army had brought back from their various wars—gold, silver, jeweled cups, bronze statues, brass pillars and images of queer-looking men, whom the people thought were gods. There were twelve of these gods, all supposed to be one of the stars or constellations in the sky. The Babylonians thought that by studying the way the stars rose and set and their arrangement they could tell the commands of

the gods. The greatest temple in the city
was built on a hill and decorated with red
gold inside. It was where men and women
worshiped the god whom they called Belus.
Daniel had seen many statues of this god,
showing him like a man with long hair and
a flowing beard. In this temple were
placed the cups, candlesticks, and pillars
that Nebuchadnezzar had brought from the
temple in Jerusalem. It made Daniel very
sad to think of the furnishings of Solomon's
holy temple being used to worship an ugly
lump of brass in this heathen way. He
saw the Babylonians burning incense before the idols, bringing them presents of
gold, ointments, and jewels, and praying to
them with strange ceremonies; but he and
the three friends prayed only to God, and
asked that they might be able to teach the
truth to these heathen men.

Now, soon after Nebuchadnezzar had
called for the Jewish children, the king had
a strange dream. But when he woke up
from dreaming he could not remember what
it had been about. He puzzled over the

matter, and at last called together all the wise men and magicians in the city.

"I have dreamed a strange dream," he told them, "and I am anxious to know what it means."

"Tell us your dream, O king," cried the wise men, "and we will tell you its meaning."

"I have forgotten it," answered the king, "but you must tell me what it was, and what it meant, or I shall have you all killed. If you can tell me, however, I will give you great riches and honor."

The wise men were very much frightened at hearing this, for they had no idea what to do.

"O king," they cried, bowing very low, "there is not a man in the world who could guess what you dreamed. No one except the gods knows what it was."

The king grew very angry. He turned to his servants and soldiers. "Then these men shall die," he cried. "Take them away; find all the other scholars and wise men in the city and kill them also."

DANIEL

Now Daniel, although only a youth, was already called a wise man, because from his childhood he had been able to tell the meaning of dreams, and the king had found that he knew more than all the rest of his magicians in spite of his youth. But the king had forgotten about Daniel when he gave the cruel order for all the wise men to be killed. So the soldiers came to Daniel and his three friends to kill them.

"Why is the order so hasty?" asked Daniel of Arioch, the captain of the king's guard. Arioch told Daniel all about the king's dream and how the wise men could not guess what it had been.

"I will see the king myself," Daniel told the captain. "Do nothing until you hear from me." He went to the throne room and bowed before the king.

"O king," he said, "give me a little time and I will tell you what your dream was."

The king promised to wait a few hours, and Daniel went to find his friends, to whom he explained all about the matter. The four youths knelt down and prayed to God that he would reveal the secret, so that none of the wise men might perish. That night as Daniel was asleep he suddenly knew what the king's dream had been and what it had meant, and he thanked God for saving his life and the lives of his friends.

The very next morning Daniel hurried to the palace and asked to speak with the king. Nebuchadnezzar looked at him impatiently.

"Well," he asked, "can you tell me my dream?"

"Yes, O king," answered Daniel. "None of your wise men or magicians could show you, but there is a God in heaven who knows everything. He has made your dream known.

"You saw a great image of gold, silver, and brass, with legs of iron and feet that were partly clay. Then a stone thrown without hands struck the image and broke it to bits. And the stone became a great mountain and filled the whole earth.

DANIEL

"That is the dream, O king, and here is the meaning: You yourself are the gold part of the image; after you shall come another kingdom, not as great as yours, like silver; after that shall come a brass kingdom, then an iron one, then one that shall be as weak as clay.

"But the great God shall set up a kingdom that shall destroy all the other kingdoms as the stone broke the image. And God's kingdom shall stand forever."

Then Nebuchadnezzar knelt down and did honor to Daniel and told his servants to bring him gifts and honors, for Daniel had indeed told him of his dream.

"Your God is a God of gods!" he cried; and there and then he gave up his old idol-worship and commanded that all his people should pray to the one great and powerful God.

And Daniel was very glad when he saw what he had done, and resolved to spend his life in Babylon serving God and teaching the people of the city and the kings that were coming about God's will.

LITTLE FOLKS OF THE BIBLE

A Question-Test

1. What had happened in Canaan since the twelve tribes settled there?

2. Where was Assyria? What was the name of the king of Babylon? What did he wish to do?

3. How did the Assyrians besiege Jerusalem? What did they build? How long did the city hold out?

4. Who were the prophets? Why did they think Jerusalem should be punished by God? What did the Babylonian king do to the captured city?

5. Whom did he take away with him to Babylon? What sort of children did he take as prisoners?

6. What did the country about Babylon look like? What was the city like? What had Nebuchadnezzar built?

7. What were the names of the four Jewish boys in this story? What sort of children were they? How were they treated? What were they taught? What were they given to eat?

8. Why did Daniel refuse to eat the

food that the king sent him? How did he succeed in getting what he wanted? Tell the story of the test he suggested.

9. What did the king find out about Daniel and his three friends? What did he name them? What were the Babylonian gods like?

10. Tell the story of the king's dream.

THE SHUNAMMITE'S SON

THERE was once in Israel a strange old man named Elisha, who did very wonderful things. He had been the son of a farmer in his boyhood, and had tended the flocks and plowed the fields like any peasant boy; but he was a good, God-fearing youth who did not turn aside from the religion of his ancestors, as so many of the Israelites were doing, but worshiped God and tried to obey his laws. So he had grown up into a wise and powerful man, a friend of the great and good prophet Elijah, and, in time, had become a prophet himself. He went about over the land of Israel preaching and performing remarkable deeds in the name of the Lord. He helped the Hebrews conquer their enemies, punished the idol-worshipers, and made sacrifices to God. The people knew by his strange acts and power that he was a holy man, and even the kings feared and respected him.

THE SHUNAMMITE'S SON

One day this old man was walking along the dusty road in the valley of Jezreel toward the little town of Shunem. It was a hot and breathless day, and there were few trees along the way, for Shunem is in the northern part of Canaan, where the country is wilder and not as fruitful as it is toward the south. As he entered the town and walked through its sunny streets he looked so tired and faint that a kind-hearted woman, who happened to be looking out of a window in her house, felt sorry for him and invited him to come in, eat dinner, and rest. She set bread, cheese, and fruit before him, and he ate them gratefully, rested awhile, and went on, leaving her his blessing. The next time that Elisha went by the house he remembered the kindness of the Shunammite woman and stopped again to eat and rest. And by and by it became the usual thing for him to break his journey at the house where the wife and her husband were so kind to him.

"I am sure that this old man who passes by so often is a holy man," the good housewife told her husband one day. "Let us make a little room for him opening on the outside of the house, near the wall, and put a bed, a table, a stool, and a candlestick in it. Then whenever he passes by he can stop and rest."

The husband was a good-natured man, almost as old as Elisha himself, and very fond of his young wife. So he had the little chamber built and arranged comfortably. In it were put a bed (which meant in those old days a mattress on the floor, covered with sheets and a counterpane), a candle or lamp made of earthenware in the shape of a long bowl and filled with oil, which was lighted at night, a wooden stool, and a small table. We might not think that this was a very pretty room, but at that time it would be thought well-furnished. Elisha was very much pleased when it was shown to him, and one day he passed by and turned into his room. He lay down on the mattress to rest, and when he had slept he spoke to his servant, whom he had brought with him.

"Gehazi," said the old prophet, "call the Shunammite woman here."

She came from her housework, her hands all floury from kneading. Knowing that she spoke a different dialect than he did, and so would not understand him readily, Elisha turned to his servant, who could speak in her own tongue.

"Tell her," he directed, "that I am grateful to her for all that she has done for me and would like to reward her. Ask her what she wants. Perhaps she would like me to speak to the king and to have her sent to the capital to live."

When this was explained to her the woman shook her head. "I would rather live here among my own people," she said.

"Well, what can be done to make her happy?" asked Elisha. Gehazi talked a few moments with the woman and then turned back to the prophet.

"There is only one thing she wants," he said, "and that is a child. She has none, and she is lonely."

Elisha thought a long time, then he nodded.

He felt sure that God was pleased with the woman's kindness and would reward her as she wished; indeed, he felt so very sure of this that he dared to promise it.

"Next year," he said, solemnly, "you shall hold a son in your arms."

The woman was so surprised that she could hardly believe what she heard, and thought he must be deceiving her. But it was true.

The very next year a baby son was born, just as the old prophet had promised. And now the woman was very happy and busy. She did not have much time to take care of strangers, as she had done, but Elisha did not appear any more. He had left that part of Canaan to preach elsewhere, but he heard before he went that the kind-hearted woman had received her reward, and he was glad. Now, the home in Shunem was joyful and contented. The boy was the delight of his old father and the idol of his mother, who watched him tenderly and told him many stories upon her knee.

So time passed and the baby grew big

enough to speak and to walk. One day he ran away from the house and went out into the field where his father and the servants were cutting the ripe grain. He stood and watched the bright sickles flash among the yellow wheat spears and the sheaves bound and set upright on the stubble. The sun was hot, and the little boy wore no hat— only a little loose frock and sandals. Suddenly he felt very sick. He went over to his father crying with the pain.

"O, father," he said, pitifully. "My head! My head!"

The father was troubled, but thought it was only a small pain which the child would soon get over. So he called a servant and gave him the little boy to carry in his arms.

"Take him back to his mother in the house," he told him, and turned back to his work, forgetting about the matter. But the little boy was sicker than he had thought.

All the morning he sat on the knees of his frightened mother, not speaking or moving, and when noon came the boy was dead. His mother was wild with grief; then suddenly she had an idea. The strange, holy man who had told her of the boy's coming—perhaps he could do something now to help her. She was not exactly sure what she hoped he could do, but she decided to find him as soon as she could. She knew that her husband would not understand what she was going to do, so she resolved to go to the prophet alone. She took the tiny body to the chamber which she had made for Elisha, laid it on the bed, and sent servants for her husband. He came in from the fields, very sad to hear that his loved son was dead, and ready to comfort his wife. But she did not ask for comfort. What she did ask surprised him greatly.

"Send me one of the servants and one of the asses," she said. "I wish to see the holy man who used to come here."

"Why do you want to go to him to-day?" asked her husband. "It is not Sunday."

"It is best," she said, firmly, but would not explain any further. So he asked nothing more, gave her the servant and the ass as she had asked, and watched her drive away.

Down the lonely valley of Jezreel they hurried, by towns, along the river, until at last they came to Mount Carmel, standing tall and snow-topped above the blue, blue sea. It was here that she had been told she would find Elisha. And, sure enough, before she had come to the mountain she saw the servant Gehazi coming to meet her.

"My master told me to ask you whether you and all your family were well," he said to her.

The woman hardly heard him, so anxious was she to reach the prophet himself. She nodded absently. "Yes, yes," she cried. "We are well."

Then she sprang down from the weary ass and ran to meet Elisha on foot, sobbing and clasping him frantically around the knees. Gehazi was about to push her away from the old man, but he shook his head.

"Let her alone," he said. "She seems to be in trouble, but I do not know what it is."

"My boy, my boy, he is dead," cried the poor mother. "I was so happy when he came to me, and now I have lost him."

The prophet turned to his servant. "Take my staff and go straight to Shunem," he said. "Lay it on the face of the child and see whether it will awaken him."

"No, no!" cried the mother, wildly. "I will not leave you here—come with us and see my child."

Elisha thought a while, then arose and went back with her to Shunem. The servant arrived first at the house, and, as his master had told him, went in and laid his long walking stick gently on the little boy's face. The child did not move. Then Gehazi bent over the mattress and spoke to him, but the boy did not hear or answer; he only lay stiff and cold as Gehazi had found him. So the servant went out to the gate to meet the others and shook his head sadly.

ELISHA AND THE SHUNAMMITE'S SON